Our Day Out

'Our Day Out' is a play written for television.
In this unit, you will improve your skills as:

SPEAKERS AND LISTENERS

by acting out scenes
by discussing the ideas in the play

READERS

by studying scenes
by finding evidence in the play to support your views

WRITERS

by writing scripts and letters
by writing as if you were a character in the play

WHAT MIGHT HAPPEN?

When you read a story you make guesses about what might happen. First guesses are based on the title and the information given on the cover.

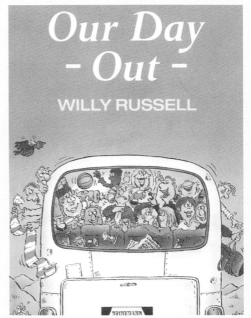

- Look at the cover. Which of the following events do you think are *likely* to happen?

1 The bus crashes.
2 The bus driver goes mad.
3 The bus is hijacked.
4 Someone is travel sick.
5 A teacher loses his temper and hits a child.
6 The children visit a zoo and steal the animals.
7 The children ask to visit an interesting church.
8 They all go to the beach.
9 Good fun, but not much learning.

- Make three columns:

Likely	Possible	Unlikely

- Place each of the events in one of the columns. Add one idea of your own to each column. Compare your answers with other groups.

ABOUT THE AUTHOR

WILLY RUSSELL AND SCHOOL

Willy Russell left school at 15 to work as a hairdresser. He worked in factories before deciding to go back to college, five years later.

When he went back, the Principal said to him, 'What makes you think we should give you a chance? You buggered it up in school; you'll bugger it up here. Now get out.'

Russell was angry. He went to the council. He asked if there was anywhere else he could try, but they said no.

Just then, he saw a sign on the wall which said, 'Chilworth County College – full time courses.' 'Why didn't you tell me? I could have walked out and not seen it!' cried Russell.

He went straight to Chilworth. The Deputy could see that he was upset.

'What's the problem?' he said to Russell. 'Tell me about it.'

Willy Russell went from total anger to total relief. At last someone was taking him seriously.

THE IDEA FOR THE PLAY

Later, Willy Russell worked as a teacher in a secondary school in Liverpool. One day, he and another teacher, Dorothy King, took their pupils on a trip to Conwy Castle in North Wales. At the last minute a strict Deputy Head joined the trip. During the trip, the Deputy Head relaxed and enjoyed himself. But when he got back, he went back to his old self.

The play takes place in Liverpool, which is famous for its football teams and *The Beatles*, but now there is a lot of unemployment. The children in the play come from poor homes.

- Think about Willy Russell's life. What feelings would he have about teachers and education?

- What reasons might Willy Russell have for writing a play about children who find learning difficult?

SCHOOL TRIPS

The play is about a school trip to Conwy Castle.

- Talk about school trips you have been on.
  Discuss:
  - how you felt before the visit
  - the journey
  - the place
  - coming home
  - what you learnt.
- What makes a good school trip?

Conwy Castle in North Wales

The pupils on this school trip travel from Liverpool to Conwy Castle in Wales.

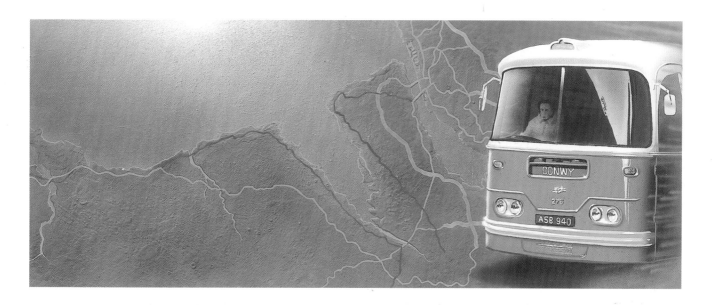

Friday 6th June

Today we went to Conwy Castle. It is in North Wales. It was very big and we went to the top of every turret. It was a bit scary.

We then went to the beach. It was very sandy and we played football.

Mrs Kay and the teachers were great. We even stopped off at the fair. We were dead tired when we got home.

- Plan a route from Liverpool to Conwy Castle. Use an atlas to help you.
- Which towns would you go through?
- What kind of views would you see on the way?
- Which parts of the journey would be most interesting?

ARRIVING AT SCHOOL

Watch the play up to where the coach driver gives the kids money for sweets (Scenes 1–4). In this part of the play the kids arrive at school ready for their trip. The Head asks Mr Briggs, another teacher, to go along on the trip because he doesn't trust Mrs Kay to keep the class in control.

In a television play, the things you *see* are as important as the words you *hear*. Look at the street scene at the beginning.

• What can you see that tells you:

– where the play is set?

– what kind of kids they are?

CAROL

We have been introduced to a character called Carol.

She is a pupil at the school.

• What can you tell about Carol? Use the sentence starters below and make up some of your own:

The fact that Carol is carrying a carrier bag tells us…

The fact that Carol is eating her sandwich might tell us that…

The way she talks tells us…

What she says tells us…

THE TEACHERS

Watch the opening again, but pay special attention
to Mrs Kay and Mr Briggs.

MRS KAY

• The grid below shows what we find out from the things she
says and does. Copy the page and fill in the gaps.

What she says/does	shows	What it shows
'Now those who have got permission to come on this trip but haven't yet paid, I want you to come over here.'	shows	that Mrs Kay is a good organiser.
'Maurice, come away from that road will you!'	shows	
Mrs Kay lets Reilly go on the trip even though he is no longer in her class.	shows	
	shows	that Mrs Kay is a successful teacher.
	shows	that Mrs Kay is well aware of the tricks that kids can play on teachers.
Mrs Kay carefully explains to Carol where they are going.	shows	
	shows	that Mrs Kay knows how to get round people.
Mrs Kay lets the kids take lemonade and chocolate on the coach.	shows	

Mr Briggs

- Make your own grid for Mr Briggs. Add examples of your own.

What he says/does	shows	What it shows
'She always reminds me of a mother hen rather than a teacher.'	*shows*	*that Mr Briggs does not approve of Mrs Kay's approach to teaching*

Mrs Kay gets her way

Read aloud the part in Scene 4 where Mrs Kay has a word with the driver.

- Discuss the conversation and think about:
  - how she makes him feel
  - what words she chooses to make him feel sorry for the kids
  - whether she's telling the truth.

Role play

- Split into groups of three or four. One of you must be a doorkeeper, and the rest plead to be allowed in. Make up your own story. For example, you forgot your tickets to the disco.

- Act out your role play. The rest of the class could give you marks out of ten for the best sob story.

- Discuss how people:
  - try to get their own way
  - change their voice
  - choose their words.

THE JOURNEY

Watch the play up to where they stop at the café (Scenes 5–7). Mr Briggs gets on the coach. He yells at the kids to behave. He is very different from Mrs Kay, who lets the pupils do as they please. During the journey we learn more about the lives of the pupils outside school.

WHO'S WHO?

Carol
Age 13

Brian Reilly
Age 15
Used to be in Progress Class

Linda Croxley
Age 15

Andrews
Age 13

- Copy the outlines of pupils. Underneath write down the things we learn about them in this part of the play. For example, Brian used to be in the Progress Class.

TOWN AND COUNTRY

One of the themes in the play is the contrast between the town and country. Read this conversation.

CAROL, who is sitting next to MRS KAY, is staring out of the window.

Carol   Isn't it horrible, eh, miss?

Mrs Kay   Mm?

Carol   Y' know … all the thingy like. The dirt an' that. *(pause)* I like them nice places.

Mrs Kay   What places?

Carol   Y' know them places on the telly. Where they have gardens an' trees outside an' that.

Mrs Kay   You've got trees in Pilot Street, haven't you?

Carol   We did have till last bommy night – the kids chopped 'em all down an' burnt them all. *(pause)* Miss, y' know when I grow up, miss? Y' know if I started to work hard now an' learned how to read, eh? Well, d' y' think I'd be able t' live in one of them nice places? *(pause)*

Mrs Kay   Well you could try, couldn't you, love. Eh?

Carol   Yeh.

MRS KAY smiles at her and links her arm. At the back the KIDS are all stifled and bored by BRIGGS'S presence.

Briggs   *(pointing out of the window at the South Docks.)* Now just look at that over there.

DIGGA looks but sees nothing.

Digga   What?

Briggs   What? Can't y' see? Look, those buildings. Don't you ever bother looking at what's around you?

Reilly   It's only the docks, sir.

Briggs   You don't get buildings like that anymore. Just look at the work that must have gone into that.

Reilly   D' you like it down here, sir?

Briggs   I'm often down here at weekends taking notes, photographs. *(sharply)* Are you listening, Reilly? There's a wealth of history that won't be here much longer.

Reilly   Me old man works down here, sir.

Briggs   What does he think about it?

Reilly   He hates it.

Briggs   His job or the place?

Reilly   The whole lot.

Briggs   Well, you tell him to stop and have a look at what's around him. Yes, he might see things a bit differently then.

In the play, life in the city is ugly. But is the play right? What do you think of the place where you live?

• Discuss the good and bad points about life in the city.
Think about:
– the surroundings
– things to do
– homes
– bad things
– good things.

• List your points in two columns:

Good points	Bad points

• But is the countryside any better? Make a list of the good and bad things about life in the country.

• What kind of place would you most like to live in?

MAKING A STOP

Watch the play up to where the coach leaves the café
(Scenes 8–20). The bus stops at a café. Mr Briggs and Mrs
Kay sit on a bench in the café garden, whilst the kids start
shoplifting. The teachers think that all is well, but inside
the café, it is chaos.

- Get into groups of eight.

  – two of you be the shopkeepers

  – two be the kids

  – one be Mr Briggs

  – one be Mrs Kay

  – one be a police officer

  – one be the Headteacher.

- After the trip, imagine a police officer calls at the school to see the Headteacher about the shoplifting incident. Act out what might happen in this order:

  1 The police officer visits the shop and the two shopkeepers explain what happened.

  2 The police officer tells the Headteacher.

  3 The Headteacher has a word with Mr Briggs.

  4 The Headteacher questions the kids.

  5 The Headteacher calls in Mrs Kay. Now, Mrs Kay, Mr Briggs, the Headteacher and the police officer discuss the best way to deal with the situation.

- How do you think Mr Briggs would react to the shoplifting incident when he found out?

- How do you think Mrs Kay would react to the shoplifting incident when she found out?

A CHANGE OF PLAN

Now watch the play up to where they arrive at the zoo (Scene 21). Mr Briggs explains his views about education to one of the younger teachers and Mrs Kay announces another stop to visit the zoo.

Read this extract. There are two parts: Mr Briggs and Colin.

> **GLOSSARY**
>
> **Philosophy** – basic beliefs

Briggs   You know what her problem is, don't you?

Colin   *(Trying to keep out of it. Looking out of Window.)* Mm?

Briggs   Well, she thinks I can't see through all this woolly-headed lack of discipline, you know what I mean? I mean all right, she has her methods, I have mine, but I can't see why she has to set herself up as the great champion of the non-academics. Can you? It might look like love and kindness but if you ask me I don't think it does the kids a scrap of good.

Colin   Erm…

Briggs   I mean, I think you have to risk being disliked if you're going to do any good for these type of kids. They've got enough freedom at home, haven't they with their two quid pocket money and television till all hours, haven't they? *(pause)* I don't know what you think but I think her **philosophy** is totally confused. What do you think?

(BRIGGS waits for an answer)

Colin   Actually, I don't think it's got anything to do with a **philosophy**.

Briggs   What? You mean you haven't noticed all this, sort of, let the kids roam wild, don't check them attitude?

Colin   Of course I've noticed it. But she's like that all the time. This trip isn't organised according to any startling theory.

Briggs   Well what is the method she works to then? I mean you tell me, you know her better than I do.

Colin   The only principle behind today is that the kids should have a good day out.

Briggs   Well that's all I'm saying, but if they're going to have a good and stimulating day then it's got to be planned and executed better than this.

Mrs Kay and Mr Briggs have different views about how the trip should be organised. This is because they have different views about education.

- Fill in thought bubbles around an outline of Mr Briggs.

- Make an outline of Mrs Kay and try filling in thought bubbles for her using the same starters.

A good teacher would...

I don't like to see the kids being...

If it were left to me, I would...

Being soft with the kids is...

I don't like the way Mrs Kay...

A school trip should be...

YOUR VIEWS

- What are your views about education? Do you agree more with Mrs Kay or Mr Briggs?

- When should teachers have strict rules?

- Should teachers change the rules for a trip out?

- Should teachers change the rules for different pupils?

YOUR SCHOOL

Your school will have its own rules and aims.

- Find out what the aims of your own school are.

- Do you agree with them? Would you change them in any way?

- Write up:

  a set of five aims for an ideal school

  a set of guidelines for the way teachers should treat pupils

  a set of guidelines for the way pupils should treat teachers.

AT THE ZOO

Watch the play up to where the coach has left the zoo (Scenes 22–30). At the zoo, the pupils relax. It is clear that they adore the animals. Mr Briggs relaxes, too, and the trip is a success until the keepers arrive to stop the pupils smuggling out their favourite animals. Mr Briggs is very angry.

Read this discussion at the zoo. There are four parts: Mr Briggs, Andrews, Ronson and Girl 1.

Andrews	An' could it kill y', sir?
Briggs	Well, why do you think it's kept in a pit?
Ronson	I think that's cruel. Don't you?
Briggs	No. Not if it's treated well. And don't forget it was born in captivity so it won't know any other sort of life.
Ronson	I'll bet it does, sir.
Girl 1	How do you know? Sir's just told y' hasn't he? If it was born in a cage an' it's lived all its life in a pit, well, it won't know nothin' else so it won't want nothin' else, will it?
Ronson	Well, why does it kill people then?
Andrews	What's that got to do with it?
Ronson	It kills them cos they're cruel to it. They keep it in a pit so when it gets out it's bound to be mad an' wanna kill people. Don't you see?
Andrews	Sir, he's thick. Tell him to shurrup, sir.
Ronson	I'm not thick. If it lived there all its life it must know, mustn't it, sir?
Briggs	Know what?
Andrews	Sir, he's nuts.
Ronson	It must know about other ways of living, sir. Y'know, free, like the way people have stopped it livin'. It only kills people cos it's trapped an' people are always stood lookin' at it. If it was free it wouldn't bother people at all.
Briggs	Well, I wouldn't be so sure about that, Ronson.
Andrews	Sir's right. Bears kill y' cos it's in them t' kill y'.

- Think of three reasons why zoos are a bad thing.

- Think of three reasons why zoos are a good thing.

- Think of three ways in which children in a school are like animals in a zoo.

- Can you spot any times in this section where the children are compared with animals?

- Explain the point Mr Briggs is trying to make.

- Explain the point Ronson is trying to make.

- What do *you* think?

- Pick out the moments during the visit to the zoo when Mr Briggs changes from his usual self to be kinder to the children.

  What makes him change?

  When does he change back?

  Why does he change back?

Read this extract in which there are parts for Briggs, Ronson
and Mrs Kay (non-speaking):

*BRIGGS climbs on to the coach. His face is like thunder.
The KIDS try to look anywhere but at him – trying to avoid
the unavoidable. BRIGGS pauses for a long, staring,
angry and contemptuous moment.*

Mrs Kay thinks…

Briggs   I trusted you lot. *(pause)* I trusted you. And
this, is the way you repay me. *(pause)* I trusted
all of you, but it's obvious that trust is
something you know nothing about.

Ronson   Sir, we only borrowed them.

Briggs   *(shouting)* Shut up, lad! *(pause)* Is it any
wonder that people won't do anything for you?
The minute we start to treat you as real
people, what happens? That man was right,
you act like animals, animals! *(pause)* Well I've
learned a lesson today. Oh, yes, I have. I've
learned that trust is something you people
don't understand. Now, I'm warning you, all of
you, don't expect any more trust from me!

Mrs Kay thinks…

*(The KIDS are resigned. They have heard it all before.
BRIGGS turns to MRS KAY.)*

Mrs Kay. When we get to the castle we'll split
up into four groups. Each member of staff will
be responsible for one group.

Mrs Kay thinks…

(MRS KAY looks at him)

If Mr Briggs had not been on the trip, Mrs Kay might have
reacted differently to the children stealing the animals.

- Write a speech to show what Mrs Kay would have
  said if Mr Briggs wasn't there.

- Discuss what goes through Mrs Kay's mind from the moment
  the keeper comes on board to the moment Mr Briggs takes
  over the trip. Copy this page, and fill in each thought bubble.
  What would Mrs Kay be thinking at each point?

- How did you work out what she is thinking?

AT THE CASTLE

Watch the play up to where Mrs Kay tells Mr Briggs that they are going to the beach (Scene 31). At the castle, the children run wild. Mr Briggs is disgusted and takes it out on Mrs Kay, who finally fights back.

- Split into three groups and choose one of these moments:
  1. Mr Briggs lecturing the pupils about the castle.
  2. Mr Briggs telling Mrs Kay it's all gone wrong.
  3. Mrs Kay giving him a piece of her mind.
- Act out the moment and get into position as a 'freeze frame', as if someone had taken a photograph of you. Think about:
  - the look on your face
  - where you are looking
  - your gestures
  - what the pose shows about you.
- Groups take turns to strike a pose while the others look and try to guess the moment and who each person is.
- Try it again, but this time consider what each character would be thinking at that moment. Take turns to speak aloud the thoughts of your characters.
- Go round the groups and listen to the characters speak their thoughts.

Now read the discussion between Mrs Kay and Mr Briggs,
which brings their views out in the open:

Briggs   I'm talking to you, Mrs Kay. It's got to stop,
this has.

Mrs Kay   What has?

Briggs   What has? Can't y' see what's goin' on? It's a
shambles, the whole ill-organised affair. Look
at what they did at the zoo. Just look at them
here.

*(All around the castle they can see, from where they sit, KIDS running, pulling,
laughing and shouting.)*

Briggs   They're just left to race and chase and play havoc. God knows what
the castle authorities must think. Look, when you bring children like
ours into this sort of environment you can't afford to just let them go
free. They're just like town dogs let off the lead in the country. My
God, for some of them it's the first time they've been further than
Birkenhead.

Mrs Kay   *(quietly)* I know. And I was just thinking; it's a shame really, isn't it,
eh? You know, we bring them to a crumbling pile of bricks and mortar
and they think they're in the fields of heaven.

(Pause. He glares at her.)

Briggs   *(accusing)* You are on their side aren't you?

Mrs Kay   *(looking at him)* Absolutely, Mr Briggs. Absolutely!

Briggs   Look! All I want to know from you is what you're going to do about
this chaos.

Mrs Kay   Well, I'd suggest that if you want the chaos to stop, then you should
stop seeing it as chaos. All right the Headmaster asked you to come
along – but can't you relax? There's no point in pretending that a day

out to Wales is going to furnish them with the education they should have had long ago. It's too late for them. Most of them were rejects on the day they were born, Mr Briggs. We're not going to solve anything today. Can't we just try and give them a good day out? At least we could try and do that.

Briggs *(the castle looming behind him)* Well, that's a fine attitude isn't it? That's a fine attitude for a member of the teaching profession to have.

Mrs Kay *(beginning to lose her temper ever so slightly)* Well, what's your alternative? eh? Do you really think there's any point pretending? Even if you cared do you think you could educate these kids, my remedial kids? Because you're a fool if you do. You won't educate them because nobody wants them educating…

Briggs Listen Mrs Kay…

Mrs Kay No, you listen, Mr Briggs, you listen and perhaps you'll stop fooling yourself. Teach them? Teach them what? You'll never teach them because nobody knows what to do with them. Ten years ago you could teach them to stand in a line, you could teach them to obey, to expect little more than a lousy factory job. But now they haven't even got that to aim for. Mr Briggs, you won't teach them because you're in a job that's designed and funded to fail! There's nothing for them to do, any of them; most of them were born for factory fodder, but the factories have closed down.

Briggs And I suppose that's the sort of stuff you've been pumping into their minds, is it?

Mrs Kay *(laughing)* And you really think they'd understand?

• Read these statements and decide which represent Mrs Kay's views and which represent Mr Briggs' views.

• Copy this page, and put a tick in the correct column.

View		Mrs Kay	Mr Briggs
a)	Good teachers are like best friends with pupils		
b)	Trips out are for learning		
c)	You can't do much with the poorest pupils but you can give them a bit of care and happiness		
d)	Children need to let off steam		
e)	Good teachers have strong discipline		
f)	Trips out are for fun		
g)	Children must be kept in order or they run wild		
h)	You can't do much with the poorest pupils but you can knock some sense into them		
i)	It's pointless educating pupils if there are no jobs		

• Do you agree with any of these views?

• What are your own views?

AT THE BEACH

Watch the play up to where Carol comes down from the cliff
(Scenes 32–37). The beach is a big success with the pupils.
They love the open air and the beauty of it. The teachers play
with the pupils, except for Mr Briggs who is still in a bad
mood. Reilly is put in his place by one of the younger teachers.
Suddenly, they realise Carol is lost and split up to look for her.
Mr Briggs finds her at the edge of a cliff, and has to persuade
her to come down. He saves her life.

- Watch the section again, and try to spot the signs that Carol is unhappy.
- Why is Carol so unhappy?
- What would you have said to her at that moment?

The scene between Carol and Mr Briggs is very dramatic.

- Get into pairs, and act out the cliff top scene between Carol and Mr Briggs.
- Make a list of all the tactics Mr Briggs uses to get Carol to come away from the edge.
- Explain all Carol's replies.

- Imagine you are Mr Briggs or Carol that night. Write an account of the cliff top incident in your diary, explaining what happened, and your thoughts and feelings about it.

Meanwhile, Reilly has been flirting with a teacher. She calls his bluff by pretending she fancies him back. He is shocked because he didn't expect her to do this.

In a group of three:
- Think up other times when you might call someone's bluff. For example:
  – when someone tells a big lie
  – when someone is boasting.
- Act out a situation in which one of you tells a lie or makes a boast. The other two then call your bluff. Discuss what happens.

- Discuss:
  Why people 'talk big'.
  What risks they take when they do it.
- Try writing a short script based on calling someone's bluff.

THE ENDING

The ending of a story is important because it can change the
way you feel about the whole story.

- Before you read to the end, discuss what you expect
  from a good ending to any story. Think about:

1 The characters you like.

2 The characters you don't like.

3 The problems that need fixing.

4 The things you hope will happen in the future.

5 Tying up the loose ends of the story.

6 Feeling 'finished'.

7 Feeling 'satisfied'.

- What are you hoping for at the end of 'Our Day Out'?

- Now watch the rest of the play. It's not quite happy and not
  quite sad – how would you describe it? Does it fulfil any of
  your hopes?

- Were there other ways to end the play and why do you think
  Willy Russell chose this one?

- If you were writing the play, how would you end it?

Read through the following list of events which happened in the play:

A	The driver refuses to let the pupils on the coach
B	Mr Briggs enjoys himself
C	The pupils try shoplifting
D	The pupils run riot
E	Mr Briggs loses his temper
F	Mr Briggs saves a life
G	Mrs Kay gives Mr Briggs a piece of her mind
H	The Headteacher asks Mr Briggs to go on the trip
I	A teacher calls a bluff
J	The pupils play a game
K	Carol tries to kill herself
L	The pupils are caught stealing
M	A new romance starts
N	Mrs Kay decides to make a surprise stop

- Which part of the play do these moments come from? Can you remember what they are about?
- Put them in the right order.

- Pick out the three you consider the most important moments in the play and explain why.

THE NEXT DAY

You can continue the story by thinking about what happened later.

- Imagine what might happen at school the day after the trip.
- How would Mr Briggs be feeling?
- What would the kids say to him?
- What might Mrs Kay talk about with the pupils?
- What will happen when Mr Briggs and Mrs Kay meet in the staff room?
- What will Mr Briggs say when he reports back to the Headteacher?

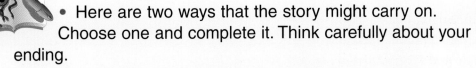

- Here are two ways that the story might carry on. Choose one and complete it. Think carefully about your ending.

1 Next day in the Staff Room Mrs Kay noticed Mr Briggs sipping a cup of coffee. He wasn't smiling.

'Good morning, Mr Briggs!' she announced.

Briggs looked up quickly. He gave a short cough. 'Hello.'

Mrs Kay sat down, laughing quietly. 'You know, I can't get it out of my head, how relaxed you were yesterday…'

2 At break the next day Mr Briggs was on duty in the playground. He had a cup of coffee but did not look at all happy. Carol Chandler appeared suddenly at his elbow.

'Hello, Sir,' said Carol, shyly.

'What is it Carol?' said Mr Briggs glancing nervously around the playground. 'I'm busy at the moment.'

'I just wanted to say…'

TEN YEARS ON

Ten years have gone by and Carol is
looking back on the day out.

> • What do you think might
> have happened to Carol in
> those ten years? How does she feel
> about the day on the cliff with Mr
> Briggs?

Mr Briggs is still a teacher at the school. Carol decides to
write him a letter telling him what has happened to her since
the day on the cliff, and how she feels about it now.

• Imagine you are Carol writing to Mr Briggs.
You might start:

Dear Mr Briggs,

I wonder if you remember me, Carol Chandler? It's ten years since I
was at school and quite a lot has happened to me…

Do you remember the day out when you saved me from the top of
the cliff? I remember, as if it were yesterday, how…

Well, I hope you are…

Yours sincerely,

Carol Chandler

• Finish this letter.

TRUE STORY

The following is a real story from a local paper. What happened is like the cliff scene in the play.

GIRL IN SUICIDE BID

Residents urge teenager to jump from car park roof

'Jump!' was the sick cry of shoppers to a teenage girl perched on the top of Charles Square car park. The 17 year old girl was threatening to throw herself off.

People in the town centre shouted at her for over an hour as she perched on the top in high winds and heavy rain.

Police called the behaviour of the shoppers 'appalling'. Their cries could have led to the girl's death.

The police were called to the scene at around noon on Saturday. First to arrive was PC Karen Griffiths. Her boss, Inspector Rob Povey said, 'It seemed that any small thing could cause her to jump. But PC Griffiths kept talking to her.

We stopped people from coming close. We kept the other police officers out of sight.'

Inspector Povey carried on, 'It was raining and it was very cold. A few times it seemed that we had failed.

At one point the girl stood up on top of some posts. They were only a few inches wide. Then she took her hands off the wall.'

For one and a half hours PC Griffiths talked to the girl.

It was a very tense time. At last she got close enough to grab her. By this time the girl was freezing. Other police officers helped to pull them both to safety.

Inspector Povey praised PC Griffiths. He said that it was her skill that had saved the girl. PC Griffiths will be recommended for a bravery award.

- Write advice to new police officers on how to handle
  such a situation. Explain what kind of approach would
be useful.

- Act out the incident described. Then, write it as a playscript:

  Scene 1 – Someone notices the girl on the rooftop and calls
  the police.

  Scene 2 – The police arrive, and work out what to do next.

  Scene 3 – Getting the girl talking about her problem with the
  police officer.

  Scene 4 – How she is persuaded to come down.

SCHOOL TRIP

During the day out, the pupils visit a fair, a zoo and a beach. Some people think school trips should be fun, others think they should be educational. Some people think school trips are a waste of time, or even dangerous.

• Consider the following ideas for a school trip:

1 A skiing holiday in Austria.
2 A day at a theme park.
3 A day at a hypermarket in France.
4 A visit to a battlefield.
5 The Natural History Museum in London.
6 Windsurfing in Spain.
7 Blackpool Pleasure Beach.
8 Conwy Castle.
9 Football Tour to a country in Europe.
10 A week at an Outdoor Pursuit Centre.

• Which of these would most benefit your education? List your top five in order.

• Which of these would be the most fun? Again list your top five in order.

• Compare the two lists.

• Draw up your own guidelines for what makes a worthwhile school trip.

FURTHER READING

Willy Russell's plays are easy to read.

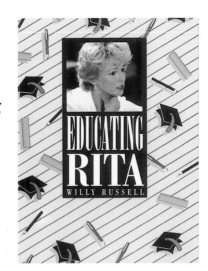

- *Terraces* is a television play. It's about people who live next to the football ground and who decide to celebrate their team reaching the final by painting their houses in the team colour – canary yellow. But one man refuses.

- *Educating Rita* is about a hairdresser with a boring husband and a boring job who takes an Open University degree course ten years after leaving school.

STORIES BY OTHER AUTHORS

- *Hairs on the Palm of Your Hand* by Jan Mark
  This book contains two funny short stories about school.

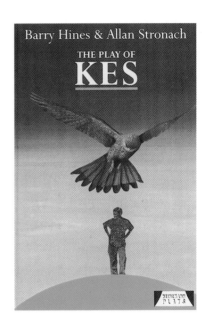

- *The Play of Kes* by Barry Hines and Allan Stronach
  This book is about a boy with no dad, no money and no love. But he does have a very special pet – a wild kestrel.

- *Boys From the Blackstuff* by Alan Bleasdale
  Plays about life for unemployed people in Liverpool. The most memorable character is Yosser, with his catch phrase, 'Gis a job'.